The Household Tragedy: In Four Scenes

Thomas Mitchell

In the interest of creating a more extensive selection of rare historical book reprints, we have chosen to reproduce this title even though it may possibly have occasional imperfections such as missing and blurred pages, missing text, poor pictures, markings, dark backgrounds and other reproduction issues beyond our control. Because this work is culturally important, we have made it available as a part of our commitment to protecting, preserving and promoting the world's literature. Thank you for your understanding.

THE HOUSEHOLD TRAGEDY.

IN

FOUR SCENES.

BY

THOMAS MITCHELL.

"Let him that thinketh he standeth take heed lest he fall."
"Wine is a mocker, strong drink is raging: and whosoever is deceived thereby is not wise." — *The Lively Oracles.*

ALBANY:
WEED, PARSONS AND COMPANY, PRINTERS.
1870.

Entered according to Act of Congress,
in the year one thousand eight hundred and seventy,
By THOMAS MITCHELL,
In the Office of the Librarian of Congress, at Washington.

THE HOUSEHOLD TRAGEDY.

SCENE FIRST.

The interior of a Lunatic Asylum. The hero, an inebriate, standing with his hands chained together,—Supposing himself surrounded by persons deranged,—Walks to and fro, soliloquizing.

Why these cold fetters! thus entwined
Around me—holding so immovably,
Within their complicated folds, these
Lacerated limbs? Why incarcerated!
Mid' these crazy people, as though I
Were infected by their melancholy
Mania? whilst ever and anon, falls
Dismally upon my ear, loud yells of fear,

THE HOUSEHOLD

And madmen's clanking chains!
They were mad who brought me hither!
I'll have my liberty or I'll die! If it
Were for cure! they'd give me rum;
I tell thee all I want is rum! Me insane?
Not I! Why then hold me by this strong
Chain in this strange duress, to be so
Tormented where such horrid specters
Hold their midnight revels? 'Tis
Madness! let me go hence; sunder
These vile chains: O ye gods; I must
Have rum!

Enter the inebriate's Father's ghost, and addresses him.

Son, silence! cease now thy raving!
List once again to thy Father's voice! 'Tis
Its last sepulchral message! These
Hallucinations that now torment thee,
And so fearfully wreck thy stormy brain,
And on its mental canvas sketch wild
And furious pictures, of terrific magnitude,
And alarming apprehension, are those of

Which I forewarned thee, ere the huge
Tyrant of the grave raised his rapacious
Arm against these silvered locks, and
Ere that which this ethereal apparition
Represents were entombed in yon
Marble sepulchre. Oh thou erring
Child! how oft, in the still watches
Of the night, have I pursued thee, with
Wearied and faltering footsteps, into
Subterranean dens, where thou and
Thy confederates, riotously, to the wine-god,
Sang devotional songs; making night
Hideous—the cheek of innocence turn
Pale, and the heart of the uninitiated quake
With fear! Have I not heard thee utter
Groans of mania? Thy once proud heart,
With irregular pulsations, bleed at every
Pore, and, from its gushing fountain, send
Forth piteous cries, whose sharp and fiery
Pointed shafts stung to anguish, and
Measureless disappointment, this Fatherly

Bosom, as though transpierced by a whole
  quiver
Of venomously pointed lancets, all
Prepared for the occasion? O thou fallen
Fragment of manhood! hast thou not seen
These gray hairs wet with midnight
Dews, when from thy congenial spirits
I had brought thee forth, and when the
Intrusive fiends, that had so tortured
And calamitously hurled from its
Throne thy reason, had momently,
Like the wild billow in the passing
Tempest, sank to peacefulness, so
That thou could'st appreciate the appeals
Of thine aged sire? Did I not then divine
Thy futurity, and warn thee of thy coming
Fate, which hath, alas! befallen thee? The
Gods be witness, that from his blood
Are these white robes spotless!
Before these invisibles, acquit thine
Aged sire. O ye heavens! whence
This calamity? O that the silent

TRAGEDY.

Earth might once again lend moisture
To these ossiferous sockets, that yet they
Might drop one tear of anguish o'er
That dread figure which now stands
Before me; who forever haunts my dead
House dreams,—summoning me forth, from
Its uneasy abode, to revisit these dread
Scenes of vitality. But my time is up;
My departure draws near, hear now
The message of thy fearful fate, on which
Errand I were sent; its fearful contents,
Though reluctant, must I read.
Ere the chariot of day mounts her
Golden throne, shall fall the last sand
From the hour-glass of thine earthly career,
And thou shalt slumber with me!

The Maniac.

Yes! I've disturbed my aged sire!
And called him from his peaceful grave!
He fixed on me that eye of fire!
I felt its torment! yet who can save?
He'd better staid within the tomb,

Than hence so hideously have come;
Yet gladly I'd the summons obey,
And plunge through death without delay,
If, when through its gates I'd come,
They'd feed me with the demon rum.
I loved that Father, and ere he went hence,
Thrice did I resolve the paternal
Admonitions, warm from his bleeding
Heart, to heed, but thrice was baffled.
This strong intent, by the enchanting
Captivations of the bowl, like syren songs
That threw their infernal hallucinations
Around my will, already predisposed
To yield its grasp on hope's last trembling
Ray. And as I struggled to be free, their
Modulated undulations held me spell-bound;
And, e'en in such extremities, pictured
For my illusive fancy scenes of alloyless
Bliss. But why now these meditations?
Begone! the fatal hour is fled,
And I'll soon dwell among the dead.
I've passed the rubicon;

TRAGEDY.

The die is cast, the moment's come;
The sands drop quick, the deed is done!
But give me yet, O give me rum!

The mother of the maniac, in grave clothes, enters, soliloquizing.

How from his helpless infancy I nursed
Him,—and when his boyish mind
Like the swelling rose-bud unrolled
Its intellectual fragrance, how throbbed
My joyous heart, as, upon hope's
Brightest pinions, venturing alone
Into the dim future, I winged my
Soaring flight, and there, 'mid
Fancy's golden foliage, reared a proud
Castle of imperishable architecture.
And as I gazed on its symmetrical
Proportions, how my winged
Aspirations reveled in their highest
Transports, as I beheld him upon fame's
Highest pinnacle meritoriously
Seated, and in quick succession
Fall the fadeless wreaths of amaranthine

Beauty upon his well developed
Brow, from whose inclosure the
Noble attributes of intellectual
Humanity, like radiations sent
From exhaustless founts, on central
Suns evolve.
And as I had thus well nigh caught
The substantial fabric of my
Fictitious vision, could ye call
Me mad for giving shelter to such
Thoughts, or housing within this
Now pulseless bosom these buoyant
Hopes? But forever be the fatal
Hour involved in night's forgetfulness!
Oh that its dismal moments had
Within the grave of time been hid
Ere I drew this vital breath!
But hold, my winged spirit! and
While I linger let me ruminate
Among the scattered fragments
Of hope's desolation.
These skeleton limbs, death-froze

Features, and sepulchral
Habiliments tell in painful
Story the fathomless depth of
My disappointment. "O, I
Have suffered!" as I beheld
His footsteps on the dark hell
Of drunkenness take hold, ere
He had reached life's meridian.
I saw him reel upon her culmination,
And momentarily, by day, and by night,
Were I doomed to behold his rapid
Strides down the declivity of manliness
And dignity, toward that nameless
Thing that now stands before me.
And ere he had reached such a
Depth, this motherly heart, like
The golden bowl, broke, suddenly,
At the cistern, and the frail tenure
Of life's silken cord stranded,
And ere old age had done its
Work, these care-worn limbs,
And the tried spirit within me,

Stung by the keenest arrow in
Death's pale quiver, plumed its
Trembling pinions, and traced
The blue depth of yon ethereous.
And thou, limbed soul, that
Struggling to be free, art more
Engaged, must bear the pang
Of this premature precipitation
Of grave-yard confinement,
Into whose dreary mansion
I now return.   [*Exit.*

The Maniac.

Her musing, and her words are true,
She loved me from first life's breath I drew;
She taught me words of peace and prayer,
And pointed me to mansions fair,
Where saints in splendor, clad in white,
Bask in eternal love and light.
But now she's gone, and heeds me not;
Her ruined child is now forgot;
In her winding-sheet she's fled
To mingle with the sleeping dead;

And yet I feel her icy hands,
As still beside my couch she stands.
But though she's vanished, a dearer friend
Comes hence her partner to attend,—
These horrid hours to assuage;
Haste, thou! and quench my burning rage!
O thou loved one, set me free,
'T were heaven t' escape from hence to thee;
She heeds me not, away she flies,
Regardless of this chain I wear,
Back to her mansion in the skies,
To dwell with kindred spirits there.
Why has she gone? why did she come?
O God, I ruined! yet give me rum.
I 'd wash away this stain of blood,
But like the leopard's spot 't is there;
I 'd rather bail the ocean's flood
Than deface this mark I wear!
Bless'd light to others, cursed to me,
That opes my ghastly eyes to see
The murderous scene, the horrid night
That stings this soul with damning blight.

The dismal thought, a murdered wife,
The look she gave,—the bloody knife,
Her piteous cries, and prayers for life,
The gurgling blood, and dying strife,
Out, out, damned spot!
I'd quickly die if thou wert not.

  His wife's ghost enters soliloquizing.

Call thee, thou dark wine spirit, an
Invisible fiend, 'tis but a feeble
Epithet, as a moral adamant hast
Thou and thy confederates stood,
Unmoved at widows' gushing tears,
And orphans' famishing cries
And piercing walls for bread!
Thine insatiable fraternity, with
Audacious hands, has wrecked
The race, and over all humanity
Spread the dark pall of unmitigated
And unassuaged lamentation,
Mourning, and woe. And, while
Gazing upon God's great mirror,
Whereon human destiny stands

Transcribed, hast thou bid defiance
To him who occupies heaven's mighty
Circle, though holding in his hands
The reins of universal nature, and
Directing her incomprehensible
Movements! Yet has he patiently
Borne the implacable insult, and
Still suffered this alarming and
Wide spread havoc of his creatures.
As from his holy heights he
Gazed upon the scene, why did
Not his anger burn? and his
Suppressed sensibilities summon
Into requisition for speedy dispatch
All the thunders of his embattled
Throne? and arm the red lightning's
Forked elements with power unrestrained,
For the execution of righteous recompense,
And exterminating vengeance against
This incarnation of incurable evil?
O, the terrific and unfathomable
Offense! depicted in the cruel

Torture of helpless innocence,—its
Damning culpability is as measureless
As out-stretched space, as though
From hell's dark recess issuing,
In quenchless streams of ruin most
Complete; bearing the emblazoned
Insignia, Hell's mightiest engine.
Ah! and this skeletonless apparition,
Which to behold makes night hideous,
Ere she had reached life's meridian,
Fell a helpless victim to this rapacious
Monster of humanity. O, could I
Exhibit in all its vivacity, that which
Within me lies deeply embosomed!
Could I unfold the hieroglyphical
Obelisk, upon whose irrefaceable tablets
Are pictured the unheal'd lacerations
Of a crushed spirit and mangled
Heart, methinks could any fragment
Of mortality, at a single mental bound,
Grasp all its fearful delineations, be he
Man or woman, the momentary

TRAGEDY.

Transition, from youth to age,
Would henceforth characterize the
Youthful sufferer, — the emaciated counte-
   nance,
Palsied quiver, furrowed brow, trembling
Tread, hoary head, and languid
Circulation, be henceforth
Their inheritance, as though the
Storms of three score and ten
Winters had o'er him rolled their
Furious blasts.
Oh! that from the vocabulary of words
I were inspired to make the selection
Of those that would best reflect upon
The plastic scenery of other minds;
But the unexaggerated transcription
Of one hour's suffering, common
To my history, methinks, its burning
Insignia, like the lightning's chain
Flash, would unquenchably consume
The mirror upon which the terrific
Picture were struck; and were the

Victims those who dealt out the infernal
Beverage, of hell's mixture, to
My own bosom companion, changing
Him, from a noble specimen of manhood,
Into such a fearful wreck of fiendish
Insanity, it were pardonable, were
I to empty the whole huge quiver
And let the fiery pointed shafts
Of winged vengeance, as righteous
Executors, go forth.
O, ye descriptive powers, help my
Feebleness, to portray vividly, in
Characters of brightest transparency,
The cruel torture of a heart crushed
To madness and bitter desperation.
The night of blood, long did I sit,
Listening to the clock's lone tick,
Sadly, wearily, and forlorn,
Till midnight's passing hour had gone,
Then o'er my loved ones wildly cast
A hopeless glance, 't was near the last,
They slumbered, and had ceased to weep,

TRAGEDY.

No father came his babes to greet;
The sobs for bread had died away,
Their echoes round had ceased to play;
The fire was out, and fuel gone,
Though cold the night, and wild the storm;
The flickering taper feebly beamed,
As in the socket quickly gleamed;
The howling wind its icy shafts,
Sent through the hut its sifting blasts,
To chill the life blood's crimsoned flow,
And shrieked to strike the fatal blow.
Their features gaunt, by famine worn,
As though to want and strife were born,
The cruel fiend whose heart was gall,
That stripped them of their little all,
Thus eager for the price of blood,
To slay the noblest work of God!
But wrathful vials kept in store,
Clamor for recompense at his door,
Dire,—profound,—final, and fierce,
Must these guilty souls transpierce;
But now the light had ceased to blaze,

And o'er my mind, in wild amaze,
Passed frantic scenes of nameless hue,
Which to my mind still darker grew,
As fancy winged her rapid flights,
'Mid doleful scenes and horrid sights,
Creatures of the strangest make,
Before me danced in hideous shape.
They whispered blood, and bade me go
Back, to my domicile of woe.
I started at the broken tread,
And left the halls of fancied dead.
'Twas him in madness o'er me stood,
Cold and quickly ran my blood;
For food the stern demand I heard,
And trembled at the fearful word,
For naught within the dismal walls
But famine's meager shadow falls;
Beside, there seemed a venom sound,
In the demand which echoed round.
Its tone was like the last sad knell,
Sent forth my coming fate to tell.
Distinctly could I read the line,

TRAGEDY.

Thus dug from out the grave of time,
Whose monumental glimpses had
Dried up my spirit, slow and sad,
And almost forced me to forego
My grasp on human life and woe;
But now, alas! that moment's come,
Its dark pall's around me flung,
As by the serpent's spell were bound,
Immovable as the solid ground.
I saw his dark brow closely knit,
Beneath it flashing vengeance flit;
His rolling eye-ball's burning glare,—
With wrathful mien, and savage stare;
His quivering lips all pale and thin,
With gnashing teeth and fiendish grin,
Then, like the serpent's slow recoil,
Ere he grasps within his toil,
So he muttering backward moved,
And as a blasted imp unloosed,
He barked and howled, and on me fell,
As though fresh from the duress of hell.
Writhing,—gasping,—by the stroke,

As if by some wild orb were smote,
I yielded up life's bitter draught,
No more her sorrowing cup to quaff.
Now have I gone from hence,
And to the frantic brain alone
Appear, as though I were that
Which this supernal figure represents.   [*Exit.*

The Maniac.

Ghosts, ghosts, ghosts, alone do I behold
In this strange mansion, as though it
Were the only gateway through which
The dead passed, to their subterranean
Rendezvous, to hold supernal conclave;
I must either change my location,
Or be driven to incurable insanity.
Here is mingled the dolorous cries
Of the untamed satyr, with the
Wild howls of the she wolf bereft
Of her whelps, and the strange figures,
Which ever and anon dance in
Hideous circles before my unobstructed
Vision.   Here I'll no longer stay!

Let me go hence, where I may quench
This burning thirst for rum, which
Ceaselessly preys upon my vitals.

His eldest daughter enters soliloquizing. Hearing her voice, he exclaims:
Hark! there, she's come, my first born;
She sent her impress before her; its
Angel form, spirit winged, just
Flitted o'er my mind; but hark!
She speaks!   [*He listens in a revery.*

Daughter.
Go, draw aside the dreadful screen,
And there behold what I have seen;
It would thy wounded soul relieve,
These words to utter, which now I breathe;
I've struggled wearily and long,
My hapless life's been but one storm,
Not Gilead's balm can ever heal
The wounds of soul I'm doomed to feel,
A loved, and loving father's fall,
O, cup of death! O, burning gall!

THE HOUSEHOLD

All my passing days and years
Have but enhanced my woes and fears;
My silent tears have freely flown,
While bent before hope's gracious throne;
I've seen each cherished flower fade,
Like withered branches in the glade;
At his feet I've often knelt,
And strove the ruined heart to melt;
Implored, besought, and kindly prayed,
And warned him, that his feet had strayed,
Then but a bitter curse received,
My broken spirit unrelieved;
Yea, more, felled by a horrid blow,
Which nearly ended all my woe;
I've seen the strong man ghastly stand,
With gnashing teeth, and firm clenched hand,
And caught the savage, maddened glance,
Sent wrathful like some death-tinged lance,
Torment depicted in his eye,
His voice for flaming vengeance cry,
Amid deep sighs of sad despair,
And hollow wails that rent the air;

TRAGEDY.

I've trembled by a mother's side,
My own deep anguish tried to hide,
Her sinking spirit sought to cheer,
And wiped away the falling tear;
Her deep sunk eye and furrowed brow,
The grey that streaks her dark hair now;
The toil-worn limbs and feeble frame,
Prostrate nerves, and o'er-taxed brain,
Thus ruined by him; O, horrid truth!
Who had sworn in early youth,
Before the exalted seat above,
To honor her with endless love;
But the wine fiend's blasting breath,
Whose aspen sting is worse than death,
Poisoned the heart and crazed the mind,
Chained all its powers to good inclined.
'T was him that thus to ruin led,
And plunged her far beyond the dead;
Chained to riot, and doomed to strife,
That piteous thing, a drunkard's wife;
And o'er me cast that withering blight,
That drove me forth from love and light,

THE HOUSEHOLD

The drunkard's child; O, ghastly shame!
That gnaws the heart with endless pain;
Go, hear and see, and feel and know
What this sad soul's endured below;
Then look within the winecup's glow,
Its colored tinge, and swelling flow,
And ask the serpent to atone
For ruined fortune, friends, and home.
Say, who dare still the goblet try,
When all proclaims, 't is drink and die?
Tell me I hate the venom cup
That's drank my soul and spirit up!
My mind with strong disgust is stirred,
Untold by any feeble word,
Whene'er I see, or hear, or tell
Of the dark beverage of hell.
Dost thou wonder why my indignant
Spirit so foams to passionate frenzy?
Were I stung to excruciating madness
By the deadly serpent's complicated
Fangs, it were a cordial to the
Implacable vengeance and unrelenting

Torture inflicted by the huge monster
Of wine. Behold the calamitous
Wreck of humanity's brightest gems,
All the sweets of human life to
Unmitigated gall converted,
Domestic peace, and quietude supplanted,
By ceaseless storms of almost infernal
Riot,—from the possession of plenty,
Furiously precipitated to the condition
Of famishing want; health and wealth
Crucified and dirged by frequent
Blasts of curses loud, whose echoes
Still skirt the margin of remembrance.
From basking 'mid the radiations
Of hope's benignant beams, to this
Barren waste of insufferable despair,
While mingling with the hapless sons
Of earth, and gloomily perambulating
The highway to great eternity, to be so
Assailed by rum's infernal bandit,
And robbed of all that makes life
Tolerable; aye, and worse than murdered,

Thus cast on the bleak shore of life's
Precarious climb, a ruined victim
Of more than savage ferocity;
Yea, let the king of the forest, or
The blood thirsty tiger, or the
Restless hyena, whose avaricious
Greed bores into the very sepulchres
Of dead humanity, attack and mangle
This frail fragment of nature; but let
The protecting heavens shield me from
That of these pitiless things of human
Degradation. [*Exit.*

The maniac, hearing his children weep as they pass him on their way to the county house, the homestead having been sold by the rum-seller to settle his debts, exclaims:

Hark! for bread my children cry,
A cry that drinks my spirit up;
But now 'tis vain, all vain to try,
This is the dregs, O, bitter cup!
My lips are parched, my heart is sad,
This cursed chain, 'twill make me mad.

Heard ye not that piteous cry,—
And saw ye their last lingering look?
Oh, heart of steel that bade them die,
Their home and all their treasure took.
Accursed treasure, cankered sum,
Price of blood; O, rum, rum, rum.
Hark! still I hear that solemn cry!
Before my eyes their specter stands,—
And when I see it, then I'd fly;
Yes, I'd fly to other lands!
But that pursuing, there 't would come.
There's no escape, so give me rum.

Supposing he sees the licensed landlord approaching, he exclaims:
Ha, ye fiend!
Guard, guard that window, bar the door,
See yonder bandit swiftly run?
They've robbed my house of all its store,
And now to murder me they come.
Drive, drive them thence, or let me flee
Where I their face no more shall see. [*Exit.*

SECOND SCENE.

The interior of a gambling saloon. Characters, gamblers, a missionary with a Bible, a woman and a bar-tender. The maniac enters. One of the gamblers invites him to play. He replies, with indignation:

I stake again? ask me this no more.
Heartless, accursed gamester, no.
With you I staked my all before,
And from your den a beggar go,
Whence? to suicide and hell,
And leave my orphan children here,
In rags and wretchedness, to dwell,
A doom their father cannot bear,
And none with him the grief to share,
No one to feel this crushed soul bleed,
O, cruel, cruel, cruel deed!
That fatal die, O gambler, why
Invite me hence again to try?

Addresses the bar-keeper.
From you I drank the fatal dram
That ruined first, at last will damn!
Addressing the missionary.
Come not here, thou man of prayer,
Shut that dread volume in thy hand,
For me damnation 's written there,
No drunkard can in judgment stand.
Talk not of pardon there for me,
Its holy joys ne'er shall I see.
Not for me,—it 's now too late,—
Tears never blot the book of fate;
Yes, too late these tidings come,
No hope for me, the deed is done.
Addresses the woman.
Thou painted harlot do I see!
I know thee by thy treacherous look;
Go home, and read God's holy book,
For thee there 's mercy, not for me,
I 'm damned already, words can't tell
What sounds I hear, what sights I see,
I 'm sure it can't be worse in hell.

THIRD SCENE.

*The maniac, lying on a couch, surrounded by
attendants, raving under hallucinations.*

See how that rug those reptiles soil,
They're crawling o'er me in my bed,
I feel their clammy, snakey coil.
On every limb, around my head,
With forked tongue, see how they play.
Hear them hiss! tear them away!
A fiend, a fiend, with many a dart,
Glares at me with his blood-shot eye,
And aims his missiles at my heart,
O, whither, whither shall I fly?
But there's no time left me for flight,
Avaunt, avaunt thou hated sprite!
And hie thee to thy native hell;
Nor hence return my doom to tell.
There, he's gone, so now I'm free,
He said he'd come to summon me,
The fiendish liar;

But see, he's set my bed on fire.
Fire, water, help, I die!
I'm breathing smoke, and cannot fly,
The flames coil round my burning head,
O, snatch me from this horrid bed!
There again that demon stands,
Armed with glittering spears and fangs,
See ye not his burning eye-balls glare?
Yes, that very demon's there.
Thou fiend of fiends, what's brought thee back?
He's crouching to make a fresh attack;
Bind him in chains, nor let him come,
To steal away this wreck of rum.
Behold he smiles, and bids me read
The message most he says I need.
See, with his fiery finger, see,
He writes inscriptions sure for me.
What's those words he's written there,
Hope's chronicles, in dark despair,
In hell they never want for rum!
Not want for rum? read that again;

Yes, 't is it, the spell 's upon me,
In hell they never want for rum.
Haste, ye fiends, drive me down,
Let me wear a demon's crown,
If I may live where rum is free,
Let me be doomed eternally.
Accept thy proffer, fiendish scribe,
I 'll haste to join thy blasted tribe;
Fill the great caldron from thy still,
That I this thirst for rum may kill.
Yes, I 'll to thy banquet come,
And drink its burning, firey rum;
With boon companions ever dwell;
There 's liberty to drink in hell.
Though doomed to other torments, of hideous
Magnitude, there 's naught within the
Measureless circumference of hell's
Emblazoned walls, of so huge dimensions,
As this tantalizing thirst, which, like the
Worm that never dies, insatiably gnaws
Within me, and, as some nondescript

Vulture, preys upon my mangled vitals,
And without cessation bores their lacerated
Depths, after the ingredients of intoxication.
Yes! let these internal fires find their genial
Element, though it were in perdition's
Deepest inclosure.

FOURTH SCENE.

1. *A dark place, representing the gate-way to perdition.* 2. *Demons howling.* 3. *Angel clad in white, with a book in his hand.* 4. *The maniac, with fiends surrounded, seated in a fiery car, on seeing the angel, and hearing him speak, exclaims:*

Hold! hold! ye winged spirits,
See, he beckons my return; hold!
He hasteth in pursuit; cease your
Noisy howls! ye haggard fiends,
And let me hear his message.   [*All is still.*

The Maniac.

What's that? He says, if I'll accept
He'll grant me pardon, and absolve
This ruined soul, blotting from
The book of fate the dark crimes
There charged against me,
Make me heir of life, and immortality;
For this purpose, he says he was

TRAGEDY. 37

Dispatched from heaven, and o'er
The Alpine clouds winged his speediest
Flight, to hail me, ere I entered yon
Dark prison house. Strange, strange, strange!
But hark! yes, I hear it.

A fiend repeats the inscription.

There's liberty to drink in hell.
Away, away! thou messenger of God,
Hie thee to thy native mansion.
Bear to thine eternal city that
Dread volume; drunkards come
Not thence, its holy air is unperfumed
By the infectious breath of wine; it's no
Place for me, and though the infernal
Beverage were kept alone in hell,
I'd fly on your flaming wings

[*Addressing the fiends*]

To quaff its fiery elixir!

4

38 THE HOUSEHOLD TRAGEDY.

At the conclusion of this speech, the fiends send up a laughing yell of triumph, infusing more desperation into the mind of the maniac, who continues:

On, on, then ye burning steeds!
Loose, loose the reins! hurl! hurl!
The flaming chariot, on speediest
Wing, o'er the projecting rocks of
Dark damnation.—The fires within
Me burn furiously, all eager to
Mingle with their genial elements
Below; on, then! on your rapid
Flight! drive! drive me down!—
There's liberty to drink in hell.

Printed by Libri Plureos GmbH in Hamburg, Germany